Interpretation
of Love

Interpretation of Love

God's Love and Ours

Dennis Ngien

WIPF & STOCK · Eugene, Oregon

INTERPRETATION OF LOVE
God's Love and Ours

Wipf & Stock
An Imprint of Wipf and Stock Publishers
199 W. 8th Ave., Suite 3
Eugene, OR 97401
www.wipfandstock.com

ISBN 13: 978-1-62032-516-2

Manufactured in the U.S.A.

To my beloved wife, Ceceilia,
Whose vivid interpretation of love
is a benediction

Contents

Foreword

That word *love* has brought peace to many and yet, misunderstood and distorted, has broken many more. Our declaration of love and our response to those we claim to love are not always in keeping with each other. Indeed, it has been said that the longest journey in life is from the head to the heart. The apostle Paul acknowledged that the spirit is willing but the flesh is weak. Yet another aphorism of our time is that beginning well is a momentary thing; finishing well is a lifelong thing.

The Christian faith is unique: Jesus Christ came to seek and to save that which was lost. The Son of Man came to serve. He humbled himself and gave even when we least merited that sacrifice. As the familiar Bible verse tells us, "For God so loved the world that He *gave*...." He calls his followers to do the same. This is something we almost never think of anymore: we are called to the service of love. We are so prone to lay claim to our rights that we bury the demand that calls us to serve.

Psalm 119 reminds us that God's Word is a lamp for our feet and a light on our path. The light of Scripture shines brightly and is able to make us "wise unto salvation," leading us to the Savior and helping us grow in character and wisdom. A life that is committed to loving God and loving people will begin by seeking God in Scripture and in prayer. A person who truly prays and longs for God's wisdom and transformation is one who recognizes the sovereignty of God and the poverty of one's spirit. Such a person's life demonstrates the love and humility that is born out of brokenness.

You hold in your hands a volume of sermons from a rare scholar-pastor who combines sublimity and simplicity and truth-telling with great compassion. He speaks of love, humility, wisdom, and waiting, and he has lived what he speaks of so eloquently. It has been my privilege to know Dennis Ngien for many years. His sermons always refresh and challenge me, and I know this new collection will minister to you as well. I enthusiastically recommend *Interpretation of Love*.

Ravi Zacharias
Author and Speaker

Acknowledgments

Hamish Mackenize, in his book *Preaching the Eternities*, remarked: "We can find no authority for laying the emphasis elsewhere. The pulpit comes first. Not the communion table. Not the halls. Not the works of necessity and mercy. But the pulpit. The pulpit is central. The whole life of the congregation turns on the message God gives to us. Preaching first: all else that is helpful afterward. That is the right order." This conviction, that the ministry is more than simply preaching, but that preaching is its priority, has spurred me on to preach with rigor, reverence, and relevance, and to develop sermons grounded in biblical and theological analysis, with anecdotes and antidotes.

As a sequel to *A Faith Worth Believing, Commending, and Living* and *Giving Wings to the Soul*, this book *Interpretation of Love: God's Love and Ours* is a third collection of sermons and talks, most of which were delivered either in the *Centre's Annual Theology and Worship Event* held in Toronto, or in universities and churches in Canada and abroad where I have assisted as a Mentor. The compilation was completed while at Blackfriars Hall, Oxford University, where I was nominated as the "Research Scholar in Theology." I am indebted to the scholars at Oxford, especially Fr. Timothy Radcliff of Blackfriars Hall, with whom I consulted and interacted personally on various topics. I am keenly aware that much could be said in a different way and perhaps better. I impute any lapses in this book to none but myself, as I learn to write in a manner that meets with the minds and hearts of my thinking readers.

Special thanks must be extended to Dr. Matthew Knell of the London School of Theology in England, for undertaking the arduous task of editing the texts and preparing them for publication, culminating in a better production as the outcome; to Dr. Ravi Zacharias of RZIM, a prolific writer and an outstanding apologist, for his willingness to provide an encouraging foreword; to Dr. Ken Gamble, an intimate friend, for his unfailing support and generous commendation; and to many pastors, students, and colleagues, for showing me how to be an interpretation of love.

Praise be Unto God!

Dennis Ngien,
Professor of Systematic Theology,
Tyndale University College & Seminary, Toronto, Canada
October 01, 2012

1

An Interpretation of Love
(Philemon 8–18)

Over ten years ago, a very well-intentioned and elderly sister posed a question to me: "Dennis, you have preached many sermons on love. Is your life an interpretation of love? An illustration of love? Or is your life merely an instruction of love?" What a sharp and relevant question!

I have thought a lot about that question ever since. It is so easy to talk about love and sing about love. But are you an interpretation or illustration of love? When people see you, would they say, "Look, there is real love not only instructed, but illustrated; not only taught, but caught."? Do they see a love so crystal-clear that people applaud it and are drawn to it? Love is better felt than told; caught than taught; illustrated than instructed; interpreted than specu-lated. Without suspicion and speculation, people know who we really are.

St. Paul is a giant of the faith, almighty thinker that he was. But Paul was also an example of love. He illustrated love vividly in the way that he treated both his co-workers and those who made mistakes.

What was the historical context of the book of Philemon? The book has three main characters: Philemon, the master; Onesimus, the runaway slave; and St. Paul. Onesimus was guilty of stealing from his master, Philemon. Through the ministry of St. Paul, Onesimus had become a Christian and his life had been deeply transformed. Paul now was sending him back to his master, and so he wrote this brief letter, full of affection.

Love is not illustrated and interpreted in commanding, but in respecting others (v.8–10)

St. Paul had the authority to command Philemon to welcome back Onesimus, his runaway slave. Instead he wrote a letter to Philemon, not commanding him to do anything, not threatening or warning or imposing or insisting on what Philemon ought to do with the runaway slave. Rather, he wrote a letter appealing, on the basis of love (9–10), for Philemon to forgive Onesimus and receive him back into his house.

In verse 9, Paul wrote: "I appeal to you on the basis of love," not on the basis of his authority. Again in verse 10, Paul stressed: "I appeal for my spiritual son Onesimus." Do you see how sensitive Paul was towards his co-worker? He merely made a humble request on behalf of the runaway slave, and left the final decision to Philemon. That is true love manifested and interpreted–Paul did not command, but sought to respect the other.

There are people who feel they have to command because they think that through this they command trust or respect out of people, but yet the result is just the opposite. Some made unreasonable demands because they think that they are indispensable or irreplaceable, and so they feel able to do or say anything without considering the feelings of others. Still others enjoy being in command because they are afraid of losing power or control.

After one week of marriage, a highly-chauvinistic husband came to the pastor who had officiated at his wedding and complained: "Pastor, you said when two of us got married, the two became one. But pastor, you never told me which one? Is her body joined with mine so that she can keep on nagging me till death do us part? Is it my body joined with hers so that I can command her till death do us part?"

Dear brothers and sisters, the issue is not about controlling or nagging. The key issue is mutual respect. Where there is mutual respect, relationships tend to decrease in conflict and increase in understanding.

Some of you men, try and command your wives and see what will happen. Likewise, some of you women, try and order your husbands around and see what might happen. I can assure you that your better halves will become the bitter halves.

A president of a company bragged about his relationships: "For 15 years I have never had a stomach-ache working together with my staff." Then one of the staff shouted: "But you gave us stomach-aches; not only that, but many heart aches as well through your unreasonable commands and irrational demands."

Many friendships and marriages break down. Why? Because there is too much commanding and too little respecting! Paul handled this relationship with great care. He was very tactful, very considerate of the feelings of Philemon. He loves Philemon, and he shows this by respecting his leadership. Look at verse 14 where Paul respectfully wrote: "I did not want to do anything without your consent so that any favor you do will be spontaneous and not forced."

In other words, Paul was saying: "I want your understanding; I don't want to impose; I don't want to give you a stomach-ache. So I am only making a humble request on behalf of my spiritual son, Onesimus."

Dear brothers and sister, how is your relationship with others? Let us learn to let go of our self-centeredness and seek to respect others more. Respect cannot be demanded, but must be earned. May I stress this point: respect must be "learned" and "earned." No one should say: "Oh, I am a leader in this church; I am somebody. Or I am greater than somebody else here, so everybody should respect me." We must learn to respect others first, and through that we will gradually earn the respect of others.

Love is not illustrated and interpreted in depreciating others, but in making others useful by seeking to encourage them in order to build them up (v.11)

I like what verse 11 says: "Formerly he [Onesimus] was useless to you, but now he has become useful both to you [his master Philemon] and me [his spiritual father]."

Do you see the contrast? Formerly, but now. He was useless, but he has become useful. What a transformation–from being useless to being useful!

Although we do not know exactly how Paul made him useful, tradition says that Onesimus later became an influential bishop. In the second century, Ignatius of Antioch argued that Onesimus later became Bishop of Ephesus. Though scholars differ on this, the key thing to remember is Onesimus was made an effective substitute for Philemon in taking care of Paul in prison. The slave was made useful, as useful as his master. To that end, Paul was an important contributor to his growth.

How can we make people useful? My mother told me two things: (a) develop an eye that penetrates into the inner being, an eye to see the inner hurts or pain; and (b) develop a heart that feels their hurts in order to stand by and encourage them.

My mother used to caution me: "Your eyes are big, but not good enough. Pray that God will give you a penetrating eye, and a compassionate heart. Only then will you have many students or followers."

St. Paul had a penetrating eye and compassionate heart–the two things that are needed to be an encourager. Paul saw the inner struggles of the young Timothy and felt his inner struggles. So he wrote two letters to Timothy in order to encourage him.

Likewise, Paul might have felt the burden that Onesimus carried—the burden of guilt, for he had stolen from his master. Paul might have seen his pain and his regrets for this past evil deed. Certainly he stood by him, to encourage him and to make him useful. In the hands of an encourager like Paul, the insignificant Onesimus has become significant; the weak has been made strong; the useless has become useful, as useful as Philemon. This is made clear in verse 13, where Paul said: "I would have liked to keep him so that he could take your place in helping me." Paul would prefer to keep Onesimus with him as his servant, but Roman law requires that he be returned to Philemon, his owner.

Brothers and sisters, we can be very busy in church ministries, and this can make us blind and numb to the struggles, disappointments, burdens, or hurt that people carry. Let this be our prayer: "Oh God, restore my sight, so that I can see what others do not see, and feel what others feel." The one possessed of a penetrating eye, coupled with a compassionate heart could interpret, and thus be an effective agency of love.

Love is not illustrated in being calculative, but in being generous or magnanimous (v. 12–18)

There are two sorts of people: big people and little people. Little people have little hearts, so little that they cannot contain anyone else. These people have very little influence on others. But big people have big hearts. A magnanimous person has a big heart, a heart big enough to take in the mistakes of others, the differences in others, the struggles of others.

St. Paul could have thought: "How can I associate with someone with a criminal record? That would be a threat to my reputation; a hindrance to my image as a leader." Instead Paul had a big heart–a heart big enough to contain all sorts of people. In Romans 16, there is a long catalogue of names of people Paul is concerned for, over 30 names in that one chapter–including the rich and the poor, the old and the young, Jews and Gentles, educated and uneducated, male and female, masters and slaves; even Onesimus the criminal was in his heart.

Look at verse 12 of Philemon: Paul called Onesimus "my very heart." In verse 16, Paul regarded him as better than a slave, as a "dear brother," "a partner" (v.17). Verse 18 reads, "if Onesimus owes you anything, charge it to my account." In other words, he is generous enough to pay for anything so that Onesimus can be accepted by his master. What a big heart he has!

The word "charge" has to do with the doctrine of justification by faith, according to which Christ's righteousness is charged unto us sinners, and our sins are charged unto Christ. This is a joyous exchange, said Luther, because Christ's righteousness is given to us in exchange for our sin. It is not by our righteousness that we are set right by God, but by Christ's righteousness, that by which we are liberated. He paid the debt of sin in order that we might be forgiven. Having been struck by this gospel of joyous exchange, Paul now applies this to his relationship with Onesimus. He said: "Charge his debt into my account." Just as Christ paid the debt to liberate us, so also Paul paid the debt to purchase Onesimus. This is magnanimity made manifest in Paul's dealing with a repentant slave.

Are you generous towards others who wrong you? A generous person accepts people who do not measure up or who have deficiencies. Have you ever been treated with generosity? If so, let us be generous towards those who are forgiving and generous towards us.

A replay of the 1965 Wimbledon tennis final was on TV. In it, there was a little incident that was very interesting. On a player's second service, the linesman called, "fault." The player disagreed, thinking that his service hit right on the line, and was thus not a fault. The player protested, but the umpire supported the linesman's decision, and so the player lost the point.

However, the opponent also felt that the player's service was good, and not a fault. Therefore, the next time the ball came over the net, he simply walked away and lost a point. He allowed the player to gain a point that he felt he should have gained in the first place. That is bigness of heart, a generosity of spirit that was so vividly and powerfully portrayed on TV that the entire outlook of that game of tennis was changed; the relationship between the two players had been enhanced.

Do you know what small people would say? A small person would say: "Winning is not everything; it is the Only thing." A generous person with a big heart would say: "Winning is not the main thing; allow others to win."

Avoid being calculative, selfish, and self-centered; rather, seek to be forgiving, accepting, and encouraging, making others stronger than before, more useful than last year. If you think that you are right, then it is time to manifest a big heart. Avoid being self-righteous, even when you are proven right. If you remain engrossed in who is right or wrong, who is more right or more wrong, then perhaps you are a small person with a small heart. We have been forgiven, and thus we ought to be forgiving; we have been graced, and so we ought to be gracious towards others; we are God's beloved people, and therefore we ought to be the most loving of people.

2

The Wardrobe of the Holy Family:
Love as the Content of Holiness
(Colossians 3:12–14)

Every occasion demands a certain type of clothing. Different people dress differently, in different styles, in different colors, depending on where they are from and what they are doing. Some are trendy, others are traditional.

September 1st, 1984 was our wedding day. A day before the wedding, I overheard my mother-in-law talking to my beautiful bride. Looking at the wedding gown, she said: "Ceceilia, tomorrow you will be married. You will be dressed differently, with this beautiful gown, one that befits your status as a bride. You are no longer the same. You will have changed your identity, from Miss Ng to Mrs. Ngien. You will belong to your husband, and therefore must live in a manner worthy of him."

Since then, there has been a change in her. The wedding gown with which she was attired, powerful symbol as it is, was the beginning of a transformation that has been appropriate and natural, legal and spiritual. Likewise, there is a change in us from the time of our new spiritual birth.

Purely by his grace, God constitutes us as the elect, a holy people set apart (holy) to be the object of his love (beloved). This is our new identity in Christ–chosen, holy, and beloved (Col. 3:12). We are saved not so that we might be good, but so that we are God's–chosen and set apart to be his holy, beloved family. Because we are his, we are to dress ourselves differently (Col. 3:12–13). God's grace through the cross creates a holy people, whose very content is love. The wardrobe of the holy saints is full of love. We have taken off one set of clothes–the old self with its vices–and have put on a new set of clothes–the new self with its virtues. Since we are given this new, holy identity in Christ, which God re-establishes, we are to put on virtues that characterize Christ, with whom we are clothed. The imperative of the new self is to reflect his holiness in the way that we relate to each other.

The selfishness that was at the core of our existence now gives way to a loving self-sacrifice for the good of others, resulting in a theology of radical reversal, which is the theology of a holy life: (i) compassion instead of contempt for or indifference to others; (ii) kindness instead of malice; (iii) humility instead of arrogance; (iv) gentleness instead of rudeness; (v) patience instead of anger; (vi) forbearance instead of resentment; and (vii) forgiveness instead of revenge.

"Over all these virtues, put on love, which binds them together in perfect unity" (v.14). The unifying force, the bond of perfection, is not the knowledge of the Gnostics, but the love of the cross; it is like a belt or girdle that binds all the virtues together, and binds believers together in perfect harmony. It is the form and foundation of a new being in Christ. The love that God has for us is that by which we love each other. Our actions must be borne out of a love that flows from the cross. Agape love, the supreme virtue, is the efficacy and the life-blood of all virtues; love gives motive, motivation, and meaning to these virtues. Love does not add anything to these virtues; it is a distillation, the essence, and the epitome of them all.

There are seven articles of clothing that we as God's holy and beloved people must put on; what beautiful garments of love they are!

Clothe yourselves with compassion

Paul said, "Clothe yourselves with compassion" (v.12a). Compassion attracts; it enables people to open up; it brings healing and wholeness to the wounded. The philosopher Baron von Hugel said: "Compassion matters; it matters most." Indeed it does.

Two years have passed, and I am still grieving the loss of my mother. Grief is an expression of love, not despair. My mother became a young widow at the age of 43, with 10 children to look after. She was still a scintillating beauty, and I look just like her! Men lined up to marry her. However, instead of remarriage, she gave the rest of her life to the compassionate care of many, including some orphans, most of whom have now grown up and are well-established in their families and in society. They were the beneficiaries of a feeble young widow, imbued with a heart of compassion.

My mom used to be a marriage broker, and was very successful in most cases, but not in mine. Based on the strength of my wife, let me be candid about a certain segment of my life-story. When I was 17, I fell deeply in love with a very beautiful girl in an orphanage. Moms and dads, don't tell your teenagers not to fall in love. Tell them: falling in love is a risky business, because it is still a fall. When you do fall in that risky business, we will be there for you. That was what my mom did–she was with me, guiding and protecting me. That beautiful girl was everything that I wanted. To our dismay, she had cancer of the uterus. A young girl of 17, with cancer? My first love was given six months to live. I was consumed with horror and terror, watching her fading away from my arms into the grave. Tragic! Trauma! My mother and I literally buried her. I knew pain from first-hand experience. The pain was so painful that I attempted suicide. Yet what kept me alive were the compassionate words of my mother by the hospital bed: "Son, your pain is in my heart." In response, I cried: "Mom, your pain too is in my heart." Because it was as much her pain as it was mine; indeed, she felt more pain, having lost her dream and seen her beloved son in indescribable pain! It was there, in the mingling of two hearts in pain, the mother's and the son's, that healing began, and hope emanated.

What is the difference between a shark and a dolphin? When a shark is wounded, the other sharks attack it, and kill it. But when a dolphin is wounded, the other dolphins gather around it, nurture it, and carry it until they can bring it to a place of safety and healing. They protect the injured dolphin from further harm. Why? Because there is compassion in the dolphins' hearts! With our new-found identity in Christ, we are to dress differently–put on the dolphin's nature and manifest not contempt, but compassion, not indifference, but bonding. As God's holy and beloved people, it should be our nature to reflect God's holy character, and to say to the wounded: "Your pain is in my heart."

Clothe yourselves with kindness

Paul was no sentimentalist. He was not a man with nothing between his ears. He was well-versed in Aristotelian thought, a mighty thinker. Yet he said, "love is kind; the fruit of the Holy Spirit is kindness; put on kindness." In our relationships with those who are near and dear to us, those who are equal to us like our spouses, kindness is very much needed. So much unhappiness is precisely due to a lack of kindness.

Think back to the time of your dating and courting. Some may have to think a lot further, back to the subterranean level of your consciousness. You were so nice to your partner, adjusted your tight schedule, climbed the highest mountains, crossed the vastest oceans, just to see that young girl. When you went somewhere in a car, you opened the door and gently slid that young beauty in. Now that you are married, are you as nice to her? Do you yell: "Can't you open the car door yourself? Can't you put your big foot inside the door?" She used to be 85 pounds; now she is 130 pounds. Of course she is clumsier than before, since she is carrying your baby.

Beverley Nicole wrote a book entitled, "Are they the same at home?" Talking about prominent people and their public lives, she wrote speculatively how they might be at home. Are they as kind to their spouses at home as they are in public? That is an acid test for all of us.

Listen to a cynic's definition of a home: "A home is a place where you are tired of being nice to people." It is sad to say, but there is some truth to this! How many of us go home to our loved ones, exhausted after a long day of work? We spend the whole day in the office being nice to people. By the time we get home, we are tired, and our home has become a place where we are tired of being nice, even to our loved ones. We become rude and overbearing. Sometimes we lose our cool and our manners, and we take our tiredness out on those at home. Home is no longer a sweet home; it has become less attractive than a hotel, for even in hotels, people are nice. Allow me to say this: kindness is the best, most effective tranquilizer that can send your lover to sleep far quicker than any medication. Be kind to each other. Do it now, and do it soon, for you never know how soon it may be too late.

Clothe yourselves with humility

Humility is not thinking less of yourself than you should; it is simply the quiet acceptance of the truth about ourselves, that we have the strengths and weaknesses, ups and downs. When we do well, we know that we owe this to God. It is all of grace that we become what we are. When we fail, we know we are not complete yet, and we commit once again to God to continue the work of mortification (crucifixion) so that holiness might shine through us.

Humility is not self-denigration; but it is a self-forgetfulness that allows for a genuine concern for others. Self-preoccupation is the essence of sin. Humility is not a focus on self, but a forgetting of self in the act of caring so that the mind is focused on others–the interests of others, their struggles, their fears and tears, their dreams and difficulties. When thinking solely about others in the process of loving, you forget yourself. Others dominate your mind, and animate your loving acts.

Andrew Murray summarized this well: "Humility is the perfect quietness of the heart. It is for me to have no trouble; never to be fretted or vexed, or irritated or sore or disappointed. It is to expect nothing, to wonder at nothing that is done to me, to feel nothing done against me. It is to be at rest when nobody praises me, and when I am blamed or despised. It is to have a blessed home in the Lord, where I can go in and shut the door, and kneel to my Father in secret, and be at peace as in the deep sea of calmness when all around and above is in trouble."

Humility is a fruit of Christ's redemptive work on Calvary manifest in his beloved, who are thus clearly in subjection to the Holy Spirit. A humble person does not take offence or fight back, nor does he feel jealousy or envy. He can praise God when others are preferred; he can bear to hear others exalted while he is forgotten, because he has received the Spirit of Christ, who pleased not himself but the Father.

Clothe yourselves with gentleness or meekness

Meekness is not weakness; it is power under control. Meekness does not involve an absence of anger. William Barclay said: "A meek person is never angry at the wrong time." He does get angry, but at the right time, with a right spirit, and for the right reason.

Henry Blackaby was my first mentor, a man to whom I am greatly indebted. I remember one time when I said something wrong, which deeply angered him. He corrected me very firmly, and with a certain amount of controlled anger. I could feel his dissatisfaction with me and with the wrong I had done, while at the same time I could also feel his warmth and gentleness radiating through his personality. Gradually his gentleness became so overpowering that I no longer felt his anger, even though he was still angry. By comparison, his anger literally subsided. That is why I was not afraid to come to him for advice; I was drawn closer to God because of his gentleness.

John McArthur cited a story of Jonathan Edwards, who had a daughter with a boiling anger. A young man fell in love with her, and wanted to marry her.

"You cannot have her," was Edwards' abrupt answer. "But I love her," the young man replied. "You can't have her," said Edwards. "But she loves me," replied the young man.

Again Edwards said: "You can't have her." "Why?" asked the young man. "Because she is not worthy of you." "But," he asked, "she is a Christian, is she not?" Edwards replied, "Yes, she is a Christian, but the grace of God can live with some people with whom no one else can ever live."

"An affectionate wife is the greatest treasure," said Martin Luther. The same can be said of an affectionate husband, who is a precious treasure.

Without gentleness, homes can be turned into boxing rings; romantic dinners can become courtrooms for prosecution and execution. Many couples stay up late when they should be sleeping. Why? Because they have traded harsh and unkind words with each other. In some extreme cases, people have to depend on tranquilizers in order to get to sleep. Gentleness is the best aid to a strong marriage–it oils the gears of life and makes living together both easier and sweeter.

Clothe yourselves with patience and forbearance

Both patience and forbearance may be understood in terms of the analogy of breathing. Patience is defined as deep breathing–patient love breathes deeply. It is never wild, never frantic, never perturbed; love is patient, and patient love breathes deeply. How can you tell whether or not you are patient? Not by how long you breathe for, but by how deep your breathing is. When confronted by unfair criticism, if you are patient enough, you will breathe deeply– you don't become wild, frantic, or reactionary. If God's love is in us by the Holy Spirit, we will exercise deep breathing, and patient love for people.

If patience is understood as deep breathing, then forbearance is to be understood as lengthy breathing. Not how deep we breathe, but how long we breathe in bearing with each other!

Dear brothers and sisters, when you think of one who disappoints you, the gossiper, that rebel in your eyes, does your heart still reach out to him? Does your breathing stop at the mention of her?

I know I was once a disappointment to many. However, it has been the forbearance of those people that makes me hang on. They did not come to me with harsh criticism: "Can anything good come of this guy, Dennis from Toronto? Why aren't you growing, or getting better, or faster than others? Why are you always so overcome with fear and anxiety? Why don't you have a projecting personality like Billy Graham? Why are you so full of retreats, defeats, faults, falls, and failure?" No. They breathed deeply for a long time, bearing with me, and because of this, I am a transformed person. I am the product of those who are clothed with patience and forbearance.

Now I too learn to wear clothing of patience and forbearance. One night, at 3 am, a policeman called when I was sound asleep. "Dr. Dennis, do you know Randy?" I jumped up: "Randy who?" "Randy Soderholm. He said you are his mentor. Are you?" In frustration, I murmured within myself: "That Randy! This is the fifth time he has ended up in jail." I went to the prison to fetch him, and did all that I could to nurture, guide, and correct him. Finally, my forbearance bore fruit. Randy is a now full-grown, responsible husband, who is heavily involved in a ministry of caring. He named his ministry: "Clothed with Forbearance."

Clothe yourselves with forgiveness

A man named John Oglethorpe, when talking with John Wesley, said: "I never forgive." Wesley replied, "Then, Sir,

I hope that you never sin." The fact is that we all sin, and when that happens, we want people to forgive us. Love forgives; it magnifies the good of others, and it overlooks their weaknesses.

When Alexander the Great became a world conqueror, he decided to have his own portrait made. The finest artist was called in to produce a masterpiece. The renowned general requested that the portrait be a full-face piece. This filled the artist with sadness, for one side of Alexander's face was hideously disfigured by a long scar. That scar was the result of a battle wound. After looking at Alexander for some time, the artist came up with a happy solution. First, he seated Alexander at a table; then, placing his elbow on it, he asked him to cup his chin with his hand. The artist adjusted Alexander's fingers so that they covered his unsightly scar. Then he went to work with paint and brushes, and eventually produced an attractive likeness of the general. In much the same way, Christian love overlooks the faults of others; it keeps no records of wrongs.

A friend of Miss Clara Barton, the founder of the American Red Cross, once reminded her of some cruelty done to her years ago. "Don't you remember it?" she asked. Miss Barton said: "I distinctly remember forgetting it."

You cannot be free and happy if you harbor grudges. So put them away. Collect stamps or collect coins, if you wish–but don't collect grudges. When we do that, we are reasserting our old selves, and thereby rejecting the holiness that God has re-established.

I was once betrayed by an intimate friend of 20 years, not a mere acquaintance. On Thursday, when I found out about the betrayal, I wanted to kill him; on Friday morning, I wanted to hire a lawyer to sue him; on Saturday morning, I said: "God, you vaporize him." On Sunday morning, my mentor sent me the words of Charles Spurgeon: "Let us go to the Cross and learn how we may be forgiven; and let us linger there to learn how we may forgive."

I lingered at Calvary for a long time, till late in the night. I found myself weeping for my brother, and I love him. I don't know how this happened. It is hard to forgive, but after four days I forgave him. I could not explain it except by believing that something supernatural happened. Humbled by God's mercy, I am broken inside. At the cross the old self was crucified, and its dirty clothes are repeatedly put off. I was free again to love and to forgive.

As Victor Shepherd, the Senior Scholar of the *Centre for Mentorship & Theological Reflection*, put it succinctly: "Holiness is freedom to love. To be holy is to be human (authentically human). To be authentically human is to be free to love."

In conclusion, the crucified self is the holy self, which is the authentic self. The authentic self is the liberated self, the self that has been liberated by the cross to love, thereby reflecting the beauty of Christ and his holiness.

3

Preparation for an Intimacy with God
(James 4:6–12)

When I was in high school, I was excited to hear news of the visit of the Prime Minister (PM) of Malaysia to my home town. There was anticipation everywhere, everyone desiring to see and to be near the PM. The local officials worked together with the advance teams to prepare for the coming of the PM. His motorcade route was carefully laid out, with proper traffic controls in place. The town was lit up, the streets repaired, the litter picked up so that the streets were clear and clean. The townspeople were all dressed up in their finest clothes. The officials, parks, my own school, and the business offices were beautifully decorated in preparation for the imminent visit of the PM. Everything possible was done to give him the kind of reception that his position deserved.

If a PM merits such extravagant preparation, how much more does the God of this universe and the Lord of our lives deserve? We all desire a closer walk with God, to be intimately connected with our God. But how should we prepare ourselves for such an intimacy with God? In this section of the Bible, James provided us with several pointers.

Firstly, submit yourself to God

James stressed this in verse 7a, "Submit yourself to God." If we desire a close relationship with God, we should be prepared to submit our whole being–our mind, heart, will, the totality of our being–to Him. Being prepared for his presence requires a prepared submission to him. No king would be pleased if he discovered that his subjects' hearts were stubborn, stone-like, and disobedient. Likewise, "God resists the proud, but gives grace to the humble" (v.6). A resistant heart creates a distance between God and us; it causes us distress, and eventually might lead to an unfulfilled existence. There is a vacuum, which Pascal called the "God-shaped vacuum," which nothing in this world can fill or satisfy, only God.

Now it is true that some people find it hard, even at times scary, to submit themselves to God. Why is this? Let me offer two reasons why people do not submit to God.

The first reason lies in a misconception of the word 'submit' itself. The word has been grossly misunderstood; it has been given a solely negative spin or connotation. However, the word can be very positive, depending on the context. The word 'submit' simply means to commit or entrust. When I submit, I commit or entrust. This can be very good, depending on the context in which it is used. Think of marriage: I commit to my wife because of the intrinsic worth I see in her. There is something in her that is worthy of my submission. Because she loves me and I love her, I commit myself to my wife as a good lover does. I do this willingly, not grudgingly; joyfully, not with a grin-and-bear-it attitude. So the word 'submit' can be very positive, and thus we rejoice when someone gets married.

The second reason lies in a misconception of God. How we conceive of God, rightly or wrongly, governs our actions and behaviors. If you think of God as a kind of secret police, an obstacle or hindrance to your life's endeavors, then submission to God is extremely hard. You simply will not entrust your whole being to a tyrant whose dominion over you could only cause you harm. Unfortunately, some people have this kind of erroneous idea of God, and so they live their lives distancing from God, or even from everything that is spiritual or religious. As a result, their service becomes a drudgery, their worship becomes dry, and God's presence is not felt. Dear brothers and sisters, is that how you think of God, as an obstacle or a secret police force? If so, then God must be eliminated or ignored, or at least kept at a distance.

However, if God is the very source of your life, the very substance of your soul, and the sustenance of your well-being, if his Name is Love and his activities are loving, then you will find submission a delight. This is the emphasis found in James' letter: God is not the source of temptation; God is sheer goodness, from whose being proceed all things that work for our good. If that is the case, then get near to him, entrust your whole life to his guidance, worship him, give him the glory and honor that are rightly his. When you do that, his presence so dear can be felt, and it is so near that it cannot be ignored.

Secondly, do not befriend the devil

James wrote: "resist the devil and he will flee from you" (v.7b). In other words, don't befriend the devil; do not participate in the works of darkness. The devil has a mysterious personality. J.A. Mackay, the former Princeton theologian, said: "The devil's smartest move is to persuade us to think that he does not exist."

The devil says to us: "I don't exist. Why should you tremble before a non-existent being? You don't have to be bother with me." Mackay explained: "Because we don't believe in the devil, we are not on our guard against him."

The Bible enlightens us about the devil. The devil is highly intelligent, subtle, crafty, unscrupulous, and malicious adversary, deceiver, and accuser; most of all he is a liar, and the father of all lies. Moreover, the devil is unceasingly diligent in seeking to tempt our souls into sin, our minds into errors, and our body into disease and decay. The devil works in our culture through deception, delusions, shame, and all kinds of vices. Thus it is a great danger to underestimate the devil. Remember this: the devil, although he sometimes comes as a roaring lion, most often comes as an angel of light, deceiving many people.

On the other hand, we also must not overestimate the evil one. Because the evil one is a defeated foe, he is already a loser. The cross has defeated the devil, and so we should not be over-superstitious, finding a demon in every bush. Christ is the victor; faith in Christ secures the victory. Christ, the one faith lays hold of, is stronger than the devil. Thus we should never become obsessed with devil, fighting against him with our own strength, as some Christians seem so keen on doing. Because Christ is the victor, faith in him enables us to resist him, and he will flee from us.

Let me suggest four practical ways to combat the evil one: (i) a humorous method proposed by C.S. Lewis is to laugh at him, since the devil cannot stand being laughed at. Why not? Because, as a defeated foe, he is very insecure; as a loser, he possesses very low self-esteem. A person with low self-esteem and insecurity issues cannot stand being laughed at. So laugh at him, and he will flee far way from us and from our sight; (ii) we should be more preoccupied with God, and the Gospel about the Word of life, than with the evil one. Hold out the Word of Life, and Christ will draw people to him; (iii) let the Word of God reside in you. Where the Word of God resides, it will surely preside; it will reign, and the devil will flee from us. How did Jesus conquer the devil? By the Word of God that resides, and thus presides, in him; (iv) we can resist the devil through prayer. As Gregory of Nyssa said, "Just as prayer unites us to God, it also separates us from the devil."

Thirdly, we must accept God's gracious invitation

Verse 8 reads: "Come, draw near to him." This is God's gracious invitation. When we accept his invitation, we will experience his supporting presence. "He will draw near to you" (v.8). Notice the word "'draw' is used, not 'drive' or 'drag.' Jesus said: "When the Son of Man is lifted up, he will draw all men to himself" (Jn. 12:32). God does not act as a mad man, driving us crazy; nor is he a hangman who drags us as criminals up the hill to be hung. Rather God is gentle, drawing us by his grace. His gracious invitation should become our deepest desire, a desire God promises to fulfill. The hymn writer wrote: "Just a closer walk with thee; this is our plea." He will fulfill our plea as he promised; he will certainly walk closely with us, as a father does with his children.

God has drawn near to us in Jesus Christ. He comes to us with this gracious invitation, "draw near to me"; and so rich is his promise, "He will draw near to us." Is there anything more wonderful than the intimacy he promises us? Is there anything more delightful than to be introduced into this divine-human intimacy? Is there anything more liberating and invigorating than to enjoy the sweetness of his presence?

Rick Warren puts the emphasis in his book on the "purpose-driven life." Martin Luther put a different emphasis on God's most earnest purpose: "It is his most earnest purpose to be our God." He desires to our God, our comfort, our shelter, our tower of refuge and strength. Our God wills to be our dear Father, in whom we may confide. So draw near to him with your hidden tears, hidden fears, your joys and pain, your ups and downs. His word is efficacious, and a sure promise: "He will come near to us with his comfort, strength and joy." Draw near to him with your wounds and sadness, and he will come upon you with his touch and with joy.

When Count Zinzendorff, a Czech reformer, was a little boy, he would draw near to God by going into his room whenever he was tempted, and whenever he was in doubt and fear. In the quietness of these moments, he started writing personal notes to Jesus. When he finished these notes, he dropped them out of the window, one by one, hoping that Jesus would catch them.

I believe that Jesus did receive every one of his notes. Why? Because God is near to those who call upon him. Our God's most earnest purpose is to be our God, said Martin Luther. He is more eager to hear us than we are to pray; more eager to forgive us than we are to repent; more eager to befriend us than we are to have a friend.

God will come to our aid, if only we "Draw near to him" and his supporting presence is as certain as a fleeing devil; "He will draw near to us." Amen!

Fourthly, resolve not to be double-minded

Verse 8b reads: "Clean up your deeds and hearts, you double-minded sinners." It is as if James were shouting to the rooftops: "Hey! You people who cannot make up your minds. You are divided emotionally and mentally. Clean yourselves up; make up your minds not to sin." There is a close connection between sin and double-mindedness. It is double-minded people who easily fall into temptation because they possess impure motives. A choice must be made between righteousness and wickedness; we must resolve to hold to Christ over the world, good over evil, right over wrong, and truth over falsehood. Neutrality has been the cause of many evils. James exhorted us not to sit on the fence; he told us that we must take a stand.

Jonathan Edwards wrote about his resolution in dealing with temptation. He made a resolution:

I resolve first that everybody should do right.

I resolve second that I will do right, whether anyone on earth does or does not.

He resolved not to be double-minded. He resolved to do right even when others did not, even if it meant the loss of romance or friendship. Edwards was a victor because he did not remain neutral. He took a stance against evil; he refused to participate in lies or wickedness. Evil might come through others, but not through us–this should be our goal. Matthew Henry, the biblical commentator, said it well: "Resolution shuts the door against temptations."

Portia Nelson wrote beautifully about temptation, and how to confront it. She entitled her work, "an autobiography in five chapters":

Chapter One: I walk down the street. There is a deep hole in the sidewalk. I fall in; I am lost. I am helpless. It isn't my fault. It takes forever to find my way out.

Chapter Two: I walk down the same street. There is a deep hole in the sidewalk. I pretend I don't see it. I fall in again. I cannot believe I am in the same place, but it isn't my fault. It still takes a long time to get out.

Chapter Three: I walk down the same street. There is a deep hole in the sidewalk. I see it's there. I still fall in. It's a habit. My eyes are open. I know where I am. It is my fault. I get out immediately.

Chapter Four: I walk down the same street. There is a deep hole in the sidewalk. I walk around it.

Chapter Five: I walk down another street.

That should be our resolution: to walk away from that deep hole in the sidewalk where you fall in. Why do people give in to temptations? Because they still want to be in touch with that which tempts them. Don't get near it; don't walk around it; resolve to walk down another street.

Fifthly, be mournful about our failures

Verse 9 says: "Grieve, mourn, and wail. Change your laughter to mourning, and your joy into gloom." Here are two emotions compared: joy and sorrow, laughter and mourning. A mark of maturity is the ability to handle one's emotions. Time magazine said that Hollywood has created a generation of men and women who simply cannot handle their emotions. They don't know when and why they laugh or cry. They laugh about things that they ought to cry after; they sneer at things when they ought to rejoice. People have become so peculiar that they cry when watching a soap opera, but are not gloomy about their own disloyalties.

We might have been laughing over things that break the heart of God and hearts of others. In a high-pitched voice, James shouted: "You have been in that mode and mood of joy and laughter too long. It is time to change. Let your laughter be turned into mourning, and you joy into sorrow."

I was in my early 20s. I had a close friend who preached alongside me. We teamed up on several occasions as itinerant evangelists. God blessed our ministries, and many were converted to Christ. Along the way, something happened to our relationship. A thief by the name of jealousy crept in. We began to speak evil of one another. We acted inappropriately and immaturely. Eventually, God convicted us, and we were constrained to repent. Neither of us could sleep. At midnight one night, we turned on our table lights simultaneously; our eyes were filled with tears; we sought forgiveness from each other.

For about six months, I could not stop crying. I was in such deep sorrow over this. So I went to seek counsel from an Anglican pastor, whose advice was a gem that abides with me still. He said: "Dennis, if your tears draw you closer to God and to your brother preacher, then keep on crying, because 'a broken and contrite heart God will not despise' (Ps. 51:17), and 'the Lord is near to those that are of a broken heart' (Ps. 34:18)." God has healed our relationship, and since then, I have become better at loving people.

Dear brothers and sisters, when was the last time you wept over your wrongdoing?

It is about time we turned our laughter into mourning, our joy into sorrow. If we are penitent about our own sins, then we will be on our way to restoration and victory.

Sixthly, live a humble life.

Verse 10 says, "Humble yourselves before the Lord, and He will lift you up."

Reinhold Niebuhr, the American theologian, said that there are three kinds of pride:

1. The pride of power–that which claims a person is all-powerful and all-sufficient, in need of no one, not even God.

2. The pride of knowledge–that which claims a person knows enough, and that nothing more is needed.

3. The pride of virtue–that which claims a person is so good that he is not in need of repentance and forgiving grace.

Any resistance to God presupposes one of these forms of pride: power, knowledge, or virtue. Verse 6 says: "God resists the proud, but gives grace to the humble." When we humble ourselves before God, God will lift us up, and by implication he will lift us out of our malaise.

Dear brothers and sisters, we should never imagine that our strength is sufficient; nor should we assure ourselves that we know enough, or are good enough, that we are no longer contingent upon God. We should never boast in ourselves, thinking that we are stronger than others, or more secure than others because we had a good upbringing. We should not assume that because we attend Sunday services regularly, or help at Sunday School, or have been serving God for many years, we are not in need of divine help. We all need this help. We need to be humbly dependent upon God all the time. This child-like humility functions like a magnet, and is powerful enough to attract God's presence. It pleases heaven, and opens heaven's gates, from which grace descends in order to exalt the humble.

There are three reasons why people so easily fall into temptation. Firstly, they are not accountable to anyone, and so they fall. Secondly, they do not spend time in the Word daily. Thirdly, they never think that it could happen to them: it might happen to others, but not to me. That is pride, which causes many to stumble.

> Let us humbly confess:
> Oh Lord, I cannot do without you;
> I cannot stand alone;

I have no strength or goodness or wisdom of my
own.
But you, my beloved Savior, are all in all to me.
And weakness shall be power, if I lean hard on
you.

Finally, be prepared to relinquish the forbidden—the judging role, which is exclusively God's, to be prepared for his presence.

Verses 11–12 speak of judging, slandering, and speaking
evil against fellow Christians. Again, Paul raises his voice:
"there is only one judge, namely God; it is the divine pre-
rogative to judge, and he judges through his law. To sit in
judgment of brothers is to sit in judgment of the law. In doing this, one is not keeping the law, but breaking it." How?
We break the law by thinking that the law is inadequate to
fulfill its proper task; we think that we can make better judgments than the law regarding the hearts of people. When
James said, "there is only one lawgiver and one judge," he
meant that the sovereignty belongs to God, and so does the
judgment. God alone knows the inner hearts of people fully
and accurately. He has the absolute diagnosis of human
hearts; we do not. We often misjudge, and therefore make
mistakes. Consequently, we create displeasure, distress,
disdain, and distaste, resulting in disharmony and disunity.
Therefore, James challenged those who assume the role of
judging: "[God is] the one who is able to save and destroy.
But you–who are you to judge your neighbor?" (v.12).

God is as displeased as a king would be if he should
find his people backbiting, slandering, and torturing. God is
far away when we do the forbidden work of judging people.

One town found favor with the king. The king named that town, "the blessed town." He vowed that, as long as he remained on the throne, that town would receive blessings from him. However, should the people revolt against him, or against each other, the king would remove his presence and blessings.

Everybody wanted to visit that blessed town and all were encouraged by the strong sense of community, support, love, discipline, and order. And then something occurred. Two of the town's authorities became selfish, and sought for themselves power and fame, which caused backbiting, slanders, and malice. They took the law into their own hands. They executed wrong judgments on several innocent people. Having heard of this, the king withdrew his grace and presence. Thus the "blessed town" became the "forsaken town," forsaken by the king, the tourists, and by all outside the town because the king was no longer hailed as the sole judge, and because the people refused to relinquish their forbidden role–the role of judgment.

Are you tempted to take on the role of judge, when God says that he alone is the sole judge? Relinquish it, trust that he knows best, and the judge of all the earth shall do right. God delights in those who trust him, and dwells amongst those who honor him as the sole, reliable, and impeccable judge.

4

The Spiritual Discipline of Waiting
(Isaiah 40:28–31)

A few years ago, I witnessed a little drama in the subway. Sitting beside me was a man who was fast asleep. He was snoring; his head slowly drifted onto my shoulder. Then he began drooling, with milky saliva pouring down. When he awoke, he was embarrassed to discover that he had dampened my winter coat.

I thought a lot about that man after he left. He looked physically fit, he was a well-dressed and distinguished-looking young man. There did not seem to be anything wrong with him, and yet he must have been very exhausted. I wondered what particular circumstances in his life had made him so tired, or whether he was symbolic of the widespread malaise of our time–exhaustion. Here in this bustling city, there must be tons of exhausted people, wearied and shaken.

Exhaustion–we all face it. The prophet Isaiah knew about it when he addressed the people of Israel: they were being held captive by the Assyrian empire, and for many years they had been grieving and languishing; the temple had been destroyed; their homes were demolished; the priesthood had become defunct; things that really counted had disappeared. A mood of national depression and apathy had settled on these people. Certainly this was not a season to be jolly, since there was no reason to be so.

The very best of the people–those who were full of dreams, visions, and power–had lost their will to live. Verse 30 puts it succinctly: "Even youths shall faint and be weary. Young people shall fall exhausted." Do you see how up to date the Bible is? With all the problems and pressures that face us, even young people in the prime of their lives lose their ability to adjust, turning to drugs and alcohol as ways of escape, choosing to live in a fantasy world because they cannot face the real world. Even the habitual winners are sometimes losers.

What was the prophetic answer to this exhaustion? Listen to the proclamation in verse 31: "They who wait on the Lord." The answer to our exhaustion is not in anything that humans can devise, but in the God upon whom we wait.

However, the idea of waiting does not appeal to our generation. Who wants to wait? We are a very impatient generation; we all want to be in the fast lane. Oh yes, the fast lane is attractive and somehow we all want to be at least near it, if we cannot be in it. But the fast lane is risky, costly, and dangerous.

The push button is a symbol of our age. Some genius knew what he was doing when he took the word "instant" and started printing it on labels–instant coffee, instant tea, instant biscuits, instant noodle, instant romance–as this appeals to our generation: no waiting at all, everything ready to hand, at our disposal.

Against this attitude, the prophetic principle for our exhaustion is to "wait upon the Lord."

Waiting in a biblical sense is not a passive, internal state; it is not sitting back with your arms folded, doing nothing, vaguely hoping that something good may turn up. The biblical sense of waiting is a certain attitude towards God. It involves firstly an attitude of dependence, waiting like a sick patient does for his surgeon to work because there is hope of new life in the surgeon's skill and dedication. In the same way we should wait upon God, in utter dependence upon Him, realizing that apart from him we are nothing, and cannot do anything. Waiting involves secondly an attitude of obedience, as a waiter displays in the restaurant, coming to us and receiving our orders. Hopefully he fulfills them accurately. We call him a waiter–he waits for us in obedience to our wishes. To wait on God is to open our minds and wills to him, waiting for his instructions and guidance for our lives. Thirdly, it involves an attitude of expectancy. If we believe in God, then we should set no limits to what God can accomplish. Don't pray like a pagan, who does not really expect God to listen. Instead we should come like a child, clinging to God the Father, expecting him to hear our cries.

The prophetic approach to our exhaustion is to wait upon the Lord in utter dependence upon God, in willful obedience to his guidance, and in expectancy that God will come through. Paul Tillich put this well: "The source of all miseries and brokenness is our absence from the God who is never absent from us, but only hidden by human blindness and willfulness." Central to the prophetic faith is not whether God can be found, but whether God can be escaped. God is the inescapable reality, whose nearness permeates the life of God's people. No human situation is ever hopeless if God is taken into account. Yet it is only when we learn to cultivate the discipline of waiting that we are able to overcome exhaustion and depression because hidden in the principle of waiting are the promises of God. The promises emanate from God, point us to him, and eventually draw us to him. We are better off being a promise-driven Church than a purpose-driven church. There are four promises in this passage, all in verse 31:

The promise of a gift of renewed strength and vitality

"They who wait upon the Lord shall renew their strength." They shall regain their vitality and strength and experience wholeness and fullness. Some of us may be fighting a hard, hard battle. We have broken dreams and lost hopes; hidden tears and hidden fears; sleepless nights and shaky legs. Some may be burdened with financial needs, with responsibilities at home, with sick parents and needy children to look after. Some may be burdened with loneliness. All these of negativities in life can wear you down until you are ultimately torn down. What we need is more than simply the courage to exist, but the staying power to keep getting up in the morning to face the burdens of life.

Albert Camus said: "There is but one philosophical problem, and that is suicide." The critical question facing us is whether we should commit suicide or not and, to Camus, meaninglessness is the cause of suicide. Life is not worth living, and thus many die. This may be true. However, I would add: whereas the plausible reason for living is meaning, the probable reason for dying is powerlessness–it is not so much meaninglessness as powerlessness that drives people to suicide.

It is sad to say that there is some truth to this, as in more than 20 years of ministry I have known more than twenty suicides, most of which had very little to do with meaninglessness. One suicide note read: "I know life itself has meaning and purpose, but I simply have no sustaining power to move from here to there." Another note said: "Dennis, you are wasting time proving to me that there is meaning and purpose in life; even with the right kind of meaning, even when I see light at the end of the tunnels, my problem is the strength needed to get there." Meaningfulness motivates living, but powerlessness mortifies a person; the one animates, the other annihilates; the one engenders life, the other endangers it.

One of the most destructive emotions of all is self-pity. Dear sisters and brothers, do you look at your circumstances and complain that life isn't fair? No, in some instances it isn't. Does it not seem to make sense? No, often it does not. Is it not logical? No, it is not. You can sit and complain until you lose your sanity and balance. You can bemoan your life in self-pity, which leads to self-defeat, and this eventually leads to self-destruction. It is an attitude that renders one powerless, and powerlessness is the condition that holds the possibility of dying.

Speaking into a similar context, the prophet Isaiah said in Verse 28: "Don't you know? Haven't you heard? The Lord is the everlasting God, the Creator of the ends of the earth. He will not grow tired or weary." The God who created the universe sustains it, or else the universe would cease to exist and you and I would disintegrate. For those of us who have no might, listen to the prophetic proclamation in verse 29: "those who have no might, he increases strength, not just gives it but increases it." Let us accept the prophetic invitation to "wait upon the Lord" and embrace the divine promise that "you shall renew your strength."

This is good news about God; a sweet sound to our ears; good news for the exhausted: that the God with whom we relate is never weary, and that the Creator God continues to sustain us with his providential care. How sad it is that people should escape from God, the very source of their being and the very sustenance of their well-being! How sad it is that people today don't believe this prophetic principle! What a pity it is that we cannot communicate this message to all the homes and all the people in our land. Wait upon the Lord. No human situation is ever helpless or hopeless if God is taken into account. Our everlasting God is there at the end of our resources, as he is at the beginning.

The second promise is that of a gift of a true, clear perspective on life

"They shall mount up with wings as eagles." We are more familiar with the surging take-off of a jet plane from the runway than we are with the soaring flight of an eagle from her nest. Personally, I love to be in the plane, above the ground so that I can see wider, further, and clearer. Waiting on God gives us eagle's wings so that we can fly above it all, rising above the normal level of sight. And when we are lifted up from the ground level vision, we see things in truer, wider and clearer perspective.

John A. McKay, the former Princeton theologian, made a contrast between two views of life: (a) the frog's view and (b) the eagle's view. The frog's view of the universe is limited by the muddy pool in which it lives; the frog never sees beyond the muddy water and the pond, and is thus totally ignorant of the lakes, the rivers, the mountains, and the continents that lie beyond. The frog knows nothing of these things because it never reaches above ground level. Its view is restricted; its perspective is distorted. But how vastly different is the universe of the eagle? The eagle has wings to soar above the level of the pond and see the great seas, the fields, the hills, and the continents–the vast opportunities. Our eagle's wings cause the soul to rise upward in praise of Him: "Then sing my Soul. My Savior God to thee! How Great Thou Art!"

The eagle's view provides a truer, wider, and clearer perspective. From which perspective do you view life–the frog's view or the eagle's view? Would it be true to say that much of our exhaustion is precisely due to the fact that we are narrow and shallow; we lack vision; we are shortsighted; and we have lost a true perspective on life.

We never rise above the ground level in our vision. We keep living horizontally, from crisis to crisis, from headline to headline, from news bulletin to news bulletin, from one committee meeting to the next, from one classroom to the next; and because we never transcend these, all of our perspectives are distorted. Like a frog, we become entrapped in a muddy pool of cynicism, pessimism, skepticism, sarcasm, and negativism. All of these "isms" wear us down until we are finally cast down.

We need eagle's wings in order to rise above our problems, above the muddy pond of cynicism, pessimism, even narcissism. This raises our gaze towards the sunshine so that we cannot see the shadow. With eagle's wings, our vision of God is enlarged and we catch a vision of the almighty God on high–the most high, the divine superlative, that than which no greater could ever be conceived. This vision of the majestic God enables us to learn how to relate to the contemporary time in which we live, to relate the days to the months, the months to the years, the years to the centuries, and the centuries to eternity. With our eagle's wings, we soar beyond the nature of the present moment and set all our experiences against the vastness of eternity; we are uplifted by the oceanic immensity of a gracious God who never becomes disinterested in us. Let us therefore use our eagle's wings to soar above the immediate and the temporal, and to see things in their true perspective, which is God's perspective.

The promise of a gift of a disciplined passion

"They shall run and not be weary." The word "run" here, according to Charles Spurgeon, means, "a constant sacred persistence, a stern and solemn devotion to the work entrusted." Like the determination of a runner, it is a pure, disciplined passion characterized by "firmness of purpose and fixedness of resolve" to reach the finishing line. A tremendous amount of energy is exhibited, and the footprints remain on the sands of life to be seen by others after many days.

Disciplined passion–oh how we need it in our church, our government, our business, our family, and our marriages! Many people have passion, but not disciplined passion; they run and they easily burn out–they quit. But they who wait on the Lord will know the secret of a disciplined passion. They will run and not be wearied, for their passion will be constantly renewed and refreshed. Their vision will be preserved, and the ending will be better than the beginning.

At 7pm on October 20th, 1968, a few thousand spectators remained in the Mexico City Olympic Stadium. It was cool and dark. More than an hour later, an Ethiopian runner, looking as fresh as when he had started the race, crossed the finishing line. He was the winner of the 26-mile long marathon. As the remaining spectators were preparing to leave the stadium, those sitting near the marathon gate suddenly heard the sound of an ambulance. Every eye turned towards the gate. A lone figure, wearing the colors of Tanzania, entered the stadium. His name was John Steven, the last man to finish the race. His leg was bandaged and bloody, having been severely injured in a fall. He grimaced with each step, slowly labored around the 400-meter track, and finished the race. Spectators rose and applauded him as if he were the champion.

Somebody asked him: "John, why didn't you drop out? You were tired, and severely wounded." He replied: "My country, Tanzania, did not send me 7,000 miles to start the race, but to finish it." It is the end for which we are called. Reach the end, not the top. Wait upon God, and he will give you this disciplined passion and devotion to reach the end.

The promise of a gift of stubborn perseverance

"They shall walk and not faint." The real test of faith comes not when we fly or run, but when we must walk or plod along. It is not how high we jump on a Sunday, but how we walk during the week that reveals the reality and depth of our faith. It is the test of a stubborn perseverance that separates the sunshine soldiers from a seasoned warrior.

The older I get, the more I appreciate and admire people who keep at life and stay at it, year in and year out; rain or shine, they plod along till the end. These people exhibit patience and perseverance. They are not always visible, not always public, but they are there in the shadows; not always on the front line, but in the background. They are the quiet, secret supporters. Unlike the runners, they are light-footed people. Their footsteps are soft, but strong; they never grow weary of God's work, although sometimes they do grow weary in it. They take on something and keep it up. Resignation is a word that they don't know the meaning of. "They walk but never faint."

These are people who are constantly drawing on the resources of the God on whom they wait. They are endowed with patient power, persistent pursuit of a tedious duty, steadily plodding along the dusty road of trivial affairs, yet with a triumphant gladness.

Unexcited by glamour, unwearied by mundane monotony, undismayed by dry duties, and unmoved by unfair treatment, their faith is simply profound and yet profoundly simple. They are the kindling fires, and it is wonderful to be in their presence. They learn the secret of a stubborn perseverance. By waiting upon God, they are able: (a) to suffer without complaining; (b) to be misunderstood without explaining; (c) to endure without breaking; (d) to be forsaken without forsaking; (e) to love despite misunderstanding; and (g) to keep on believing against apparent contradictions. All of these are the fruits they reap from a life that is deeply rooted in God.

There was an article in the Moscow News about the grandmothers of Russia. These women, wrinkled and weak, walked the streets of Moscow alone, daily and quietly, praying to the God to whom they held fast. Many of their husbands were killed during the reign of Stalin. When missionaries asked the Russians why they first hungered for God, their answers were the same: "Because I have a grandmother who firmly believed; a grandmother who persevered in waiting on the Lord, pleading for her grandchildren." Indeed, hidden in the depths of these grandmothers' stubborn perseverance and fervent prayers is the hope of Russia.

A story was told of a wearied traveler. He was traveling across the land; the sun was beating on him, and it was hot; he was exhausted. Suddenly he came upon a marvelous oak tree. He sank down into the shade of the oak tree. Looking at the oak tree, he gratefully said: "Oak tree! Oak tree! What a lucky chance that I have found you!" And the oak tree replied: "It was no lucky chance that you found me. I have been here waiting for you for over 400 years."

In the same way, God has been waiting here to shower his promises or gifts upon us; he is waiting for us to wait on him. It is not a shame to be exhausted, but it is if we stay exhausted when God is waiting to give us so much.

Don't you know? Haven't you heard that our God never grows tired or weary? The God who never grows tired is never tired or wearied of you. This is Good News, the Gospel for the exhausted. Christ above is never tired of us; Christ who resides with his Father presides over the world; he perseveres with us; he intercedes for us before the throne of God above. With a God like that, we have no reason not to wait upon Him.

5

Sensible Reflection, not Impulsive Reaction
(Philippians 1:3–6)

An American preacher, Dr. Henry Emerson Forsdick, was correct when he said: "All times are God's times, and can be very good times, if only we know what to do with them." The Apostle Paul, when he was writing this epistle, was evidently in a very difficult situation. He was being persecuted and had been imprisoned. But he spent his time, which was God's time, not indulging in impulsive reactions, but in sensible reflection.

As a thanksgiving meditation, let me share with you Paul's four reflections, which are encapsulated in four key words:

The first word to highlight is the word 'remember'

In verse 3, Paul wrote: "In every remembrance of you . . ." As Paul reflected, his mind went back to the time that he had spent in Philippi, and he remembered. The most frequently used word in the English language is "remember." How many times do we use the word "remember?" We say to our kids: remember your lunch; the weather is getting cold, remember to wear a jacket. My wife says to me: remember your sermon script when you go to preach. Remember, remember, remember . . . What a precious and powerful gift memory is. It has been said that memory is life itself. It is painful to lose one's memory; amnesia is one of the most frightening diseases in that it removes from a person all the power to live. Memories can create life and hope in all its beauty.

This is why we need to keep our good memories alive because we may need them to keep us alive. My mom said to me: "son, if you want longevity in marriage, create good memories, keep them alive, for one day you may need them to keep you alive." Anybody who forgets the past is either empty-headed, or empty-hearted.

Remember to remember the past deeds of God, the blessings of God, the goodness that we have received from others. The past has given St. Paul some marvelous memories that he has brought with him to prison. There, in the prison, in that most difficult time, he remembered the loving support that he had received from the Philippian Church, the support that he did not deserve, and which he could not imagine. Paul remembered all of these, and he committed all of his experiences to his memory. Let us remember to remember what God has done.

The second word is 'thank'

Paul said: "In every remembrance of you, I thank God for them." There is an intrinsic link between remembrance and thanksgiving. Think and thank belong together. Thankful people are thoughtful people; thoughtful people are thankful people. Paul said: "I remember, and I am thankful." Remembrance leads to gratitude.

We thank God for our country, for religious and political freedom, for the various amusements and attractions that she provides for our enjoyment. Yes, she is going through economic crises. Life itself is full of setbacks or problems. How can we give thanks when problems surround us? Paul's advice is to count your blessings, and his belief is that God does care.

There is a relevant poem for this:

> Count your garden by the flowers, never by the
> leaves that fall;
> Count your days by golden hours; don't remem-
> ber clouds at all;
> Count your night by stars, not by shadows;
> Count your life by smiles, not by tears; and have
> joy with every birthday;
> Count your age by friends, not by years.

Remember the leaders of your country; remember your loves, remember those who labor and give themselves for your benefit; thank those who labor in the church and in your family.

The third important word in Paul's reflection is 'partnership'

In verse 5, Paul writes: "because of your partnership in the gospel from the first day until now." Paul is a giant of the faith, but he needed his friends and fellow-workers to stand by him and with him. He found such people in Philippi. When Paul reflected about his, he was struck with joy because of the partnership he had with the church at Philippi.

He knew that every ministry is a partnership. It is "we" who come together for the same gospel.

All of us are tempted to play the savior; the savior complex is in all of us. Have you ever said to yourself quietly: "Oh, thank God, the church would have collapsed had I not been here; my family would not survive, if I were not around"? Even a little child can be intoxicated with a savior complex. I remember one event as vividly as if it happened yesterday. When my father died, I was only 8 years old. The family was still going through its period of mourning. At midnight one night, I could not sleep. I said to my deceased father: "Dad, you have left us, but I am still here. I am going to save this family from poverty and pain." An eight old boy wanted to be a savior because there was a "*Big Kid*" inside me that said, "Thank goodness, I am here to take care of the family."

On one occasion, my mom needed water for cooking. In my village, it took about twenty minutes to walk to the well to fetch water. I did this once but, after the first round, I fell and collapsed. The full bucket of water was too heavy for me to carry. My mom saw me crying, and she ran towards me sympathetically to pick me up. She said the most moving thing: "Son, there is no need to feel sad because we have ten brothers and sisters in this family."

With a choking voice and teary eyes, she comforted me: "I knew that you wanted to help, but you do not have to do it alone. We are in this together." I have been learning about partnership from that day; no more "one-man show" from me, although I am still tempted.

Paul did not succumb to an egotism that said, "I could do it all by myself." Instead, he said that, through our partnership, we did it together for the glory of the God who calls us into partnership. So let us stay together, plan together, pray together, struggle together, and let us rejoice in our partnership, which is God's gift.

The final word is in verse 6: "confident"

In verse 6, Paul said: "I am confident that he who began a good work in you will carry it unto completion until the Day of Christ Jesus." Paul was in the midst of his trial. Yet in this terrible condition, he believed Jesus to be the best. He said: "I am confident."

I read a great golf manual that contains instructions about how to win a golf game. The last instruction in the manual was: "Persevere, never give up! Your opponents may die any minute." With that theory, I could beat anybody at any sport, even Mohammed Ali, the king of boxing, since he might collapse if I manage to hang on. But Paul's instruction to the suffering Christians at Philippi was this: "Persevere! Never give up; your opponents are well and alive." Adversaries, disappointments, and trials of all kinds, these opponents in life may come, and will continue to come. But never give up. Persevere because Christ, who has begun a good work in us, will complete it. He has not stopped working, has he? He has never stopped loving, caring for, and keeping us, and he will sustain us. He will continue to uphold us until our journeys are over. That is why Paul, over and over again, said: Rejoice in the Lord always; for Christ is my confidence and my joy.

There was a cartoon that talked about Charlie and Lucy. Lucy asked: "Charlie, tell me what security is."

Charlie replied: "Well, that is easy. I can tell you straight what that means. Security is sleeping safe and sound in the backseat of the car when your mom and dad are in the front, driving and worrying for you."

Lucy replied: "Oh, that is so good. I like it."

Then Charlie said: "But it is not going to last. One day there will be no more sleeping soundly in the backseat of the car when you don't have to worry about anything. You will be all grown-up. You will be sitting in the front, doing all the running away, the driving, and the worrying. There will be *No More* sleeping safe and sound in the backseat."

Lucy cried: "No more; you really mean it?"

With solemnity, he said: "*No More!*"

Lucy was frightened. Overwhelmed by the heavy burdens and responsibilities ahead, she turned to Charles and said: "Charlie, take my hand and walk with me." The last piece of the cartoon has them walking hand in hand towards the sunset.

Dear brothers and sisters, some of you are facing doubts and anxieties, have hidden tears and fears, sleepless nights and broken dreams. God knows it all –he knows your difficult times. But all times can be very good times, if our confidence is in him. Whom do you trust? Christ is my confidence in whom I place my trust. He invites us to put our hands in his hands, and he will walk with us until our traveling days are over.

6

Live as Wise
(Ephesians 5:15–21)

An American Preacher, Billy Sunday, said something that is very interesting and true: "A Christian can repent and be saved, but remain stupid for life." He said that there were so many genuine, born-again Christians, fervently serving God, well-known by the public, very knowledgeable, but acting as fools, not as wise in this present evil world. Or, they are educated fools, not educated wise. How true it is! How sad it is!

Every area of our society–the church, education, businesses, families, and marriage–is crying out for wisdom from above. As one African pastor cried out in the middle of the night, "Lord, give me wisdom, lest I perish!"

St. Paul exhorted us in verse 15: "Be careful, then, how you live–not as unwise, but as fools." He was emphatic: we must make a choice not to live carelessly; we cannot leave the Christian life to chance. A resolution must be made, for there are risks or dangers in being neutral. In this little section, Paul spoke specifically of how to live as wise. There are four points to note.

A wise person makes the most of the opportunity at hand (v. 15)

Our English word "opportunity" comes from the Latin word meaning "towards the port." It suggests a ship taking advantage of the wind and tide to arrive safely in the harbor.

Paul tells us that the days are evil, so we should take advantage of every opportunity, every occasion, every moment to do good, to serve God, to love and care for others. Some people think that time is money, and they therefore spend a lot of time and energy earning much for their families, yet they do not have time or opportunities to spend it. By the time that they can spend it, they are too old, their children have grown up, and they are left all alone, lonely and miserable.

Time is not money; time is life. To waste the time God has given us is to waste one's life. A wise person does not waste his time, but treasures it. Because he knows that his time and his life belong to God, he seeks to be a good steward of both, for the two are intrinsically one.

Jean Paul Richter was wise to say this: "Don't wait for extraordinary circumstances to do good; try to use ordinary circumstances or situations to do good." To be sure, there are not many extraordinary circumstances, but they are many ordinary circumstances or opportunities when we can do good. Many of these are wasted because of laziness. M. Scott Peck, an American psychiatrist, observed that the main reason why North Americans are increasingly failing in family life was because of laziness. They may want success for their family or marriage, but they are too lazy to spend time with their family. They are too lazy to love, or to do or say anything that is encouraging. They talk a lot about quality time, but unfortunately most people think that quality time is 15 minutes. How can quality result from such a short time together? It is impossible, for you cannot have a quality of relationship without quantity of time.

Abigail Van Buren, the family counselor, said this: "If you want your children to turn out well, spend twice as much as time with them, and half as much money on them." A mother gave her children three credit cards, while they were far away in Asia. Her children ended up with depression; even although they were rich enough to buy things, their hearts were empty. What children need most is time together with their parents: to love and to be loved; to feel and to be understood; to listen and to be heard.

A wise person seeks to know and to do the will of God

Verse 17 says: "Be not foolish, but understand what the Lord's will is."

The philosopher C.S. Lewis said: "There are only two types of Christians. One says to God joyfully: 'Thy will be done.' The other resists God's will, to whom God says: 'Then your will be done.'"

A self-centered Christian is a foolish Christian. He does not delight in God's perfect will; he will not consult with God about his will; he will not inquire what the Lord's will is. He becomes so curved in upon himself that no one else, not even God, matters. Often tragedy results because we think that we can run our lives better than God, and we end up ruining our lives. Tragedy results because of our foolishness.

There were two medical students, husband and wife, and both were my close friends. They were outstanding students. In the third year of their medical training, an unplanned pregnancy occurred. They had originally planned to become parents four years after their graduation. They wanted to succeed and become top surgeons. This un-planned pregnancy would certainly affect their goal and hinder their progress. Their hearts were so controlled by fame and prestige that the wife insisted her husband perform an abortion on her. Tragedy occurred when the husband, an inexperienced medical student, gave her an overdose of anesthetic, and literally killed her.

When I arrived at the scene, I saw him shaking his wife, hoping to resurrect her, hoping that the clock would turn back an hour. Sobbing like a little boy, he said: "I was so stupid. I wished I had listened to your advice. I wish I had considered God's purpose and his perfect will. Now I have made a mess, but also committed a murder." This man ended up in a psychiatric ward.

Why I am recounting this story? Not because I am better than him. No! Rather I encourage myself, and especially some of us older Christians, to reflect: "What occupies our hearts? Is it fame, power, or some sinful, sinister plot within our hearts? Listen to God's exhortation: "Be wise, and seek God's will." Wisdom says: "It is God's will I want, nothing more, nothing less, and nothing else."

A wise person desires the filling of the Holy Spirit

Verse 18 says: "Do not get drunk on wine, which leads to debauchery. Instead be filled with the Holy Spirit." Have you ever seen the behavior of a drunk? Drunkenness leads to immoral behavior; a drunkard is powerless, visionless, without direction and hopeless, under the control of the alcohol. But Paul advised his readers: be wise, be alert, and be sober. Be filled by the Holy Spirit, the Spirit of truth, who illumines us concerning the truth of who God is and who we are in relation to him, the Spirit of comfort who is our consolation, the Spirit who will guide us into the paths of righteousness. It is a command, not an option, that we be filled with the Spirit. It is an ongoing experience and a daily discipline. To be filled by the Holy Spirit is to be captivated, motivated, and activated by the Spirit so that we can do the impossible, even the inconceivable. The Spirit will equip us with a clear and sound mind, the opposite of a drunkard's.

When Jesus' disciples came under the all-empowering might of the Spirit, these weak disciples became bold witnesses; they even died for their faith. They turned the whole world upside-down–all due to the work of the Holy Spirit.

A young boy came to the studio of a famous Italian artist who had died. He asked the lady there, "Madam, would you lend me the Master's brush?" The boy longed to be an artist like the Master, and he wished for the great Master's touch. So the woman placed the brush in the boy's hand. He tried very hard to paint, but he failed. He could paint no better with that brush than with his own. The woman then told him: "Boy, you could not paint like the great Master because you did not have his spirit and his gift."

Of all creatures, we are indeed the blessed ones who have been given the gift of the Holy Spirit. Without God's Spirit, all of us would be doomed to fail and be discouraged. With the Holy Spirit within us, empowering us, motivating us, and guiding us, we would be foolish not to desire a closer communion with the Spirit.

Do you have dreams or ambitions or desires? Then submit them to the guidance of the Holy Spirit. He will provide clarity amidst obscurity, certainty amidst doubt, consolation for our unspeakable wounds. Do not live as a drunkard, totally under the mercy of alcohol; the end result of that is calamity and destruction. Rather live as wise in the power and presence of the Holy Spirit.

Finally, a wise person seeks harmony, not divisiveness

Where the Spirit is, there is wisdom; where wisdom is, there will be the harmonious expression of love in corporate life and community worship. Speaking to both Jews and Gentiles in one church, Paul told them, "be in one accord in love, worship, and fellowship." Verse 19 says: "Speak to one another with psalms, hymns, and spiritual songs." Verse 21 says: "Submit to one another in the fear of the Lord." This implies a kindred expression of mutual love and affectionate bonding with each other in one community.

When the church is harmonious, the hymns and songs it sings are joyful and uplifting. This expression of praise and worship makes a church a form of heaven on earth. Where disharmony and discord abound, even the best songs sung by the best singers become distasteful and uninviting. People will not listen to our songs, and we will find it hard to sing and worship in one accord.

A story was told about two African brothers. The elder was handsome and brilliant; the younger brother was a hunchback. He was not brilliant, but he could sing. When he sang, people would listen because his music was so amazing.

One day the hunchbacked brother was attacked by other students. They humiliated him by stripping off his shirt, and made fun of his ugly hunchback. The older brother knew what was going on; he could have stopped the whole thing, but he did not. The hunchback was in turmoil and extremely embarrassed. He left the school in grief and went back home. The sad thing is that he never sang again. What a waste of talent!

Some six years later, when the older brother was in Palestine, war broke out. He was wounded by a bullet. Only then did he realize how he had wounded his brother. Therefore, he made a very difficult journey back to South Africa, to his old home town. He went straight to his brother and asked him for forgiveness. The two brothers talked for hours into the night until they were reconciled. The older brother fell asleep. The next morning, he was awakened by the sound of his hunchbacked brother singing again, for the first time after a long silence. Then the elder brother joined him, singing together in one accord. Their music is so touching that it moves the whole African village to tears.

Dear brothers and sister, our songs today are good; even with diversities of cultures and church background, there is a harmonious expression in one accord amongst us. When the Spirit fills a community, differences don't matter; wisdom manifests itself in an outbreak of praise and love amongst us. The music of our hearts will be delightful, our thanksgiving will be real, and our worship will be liberating. A community characterized by wisdom is one where people share freely, sing joyfully, and thank God eagerly.

7

Human Needs and God's Provision
(Psalm 90:12–17)

Moses, a godly and yet an old man, was praying to God. In this short prayer, we can tell what is going on in his heart, what he really needs in life, and what is important for him in life. What we talk about often discloses what is most important to us, and what our deepest needs are; these will be part of our conversations. It is the same in prayer. What we pray about is important to us, and is indeed what we need; and these areas will be a key part of our communion with God. What we pray about must crucially reflect our needs, which God will provide for.

Let us look at Moses' prayer, and see through this what our deepest needs are. Not only can we learn from Moses how we should pray, but also what we should be seeking in life.

The need for divine wisdom

In verse 12, Moses prays: "Lord, teach us to number our days, so that we may attain a heart of wisdom." Moses' deepest need is not knowledge, but wisdom–a heart full of wisdom, and a mind full of knowledge. A British philosopher put this well: "This world and this age is filled with knowledge, but lacking in wisdom." What is Moses' deepest need? The top priority is not money, nor fame, power, success, or the freedom to say or do anything that he wants; these are not his greatest needs. His most urgent need is this: for his life to be guided by divine wisdom, not by worldly wisdom.

We should never confuse knowledge with wisdom. Many people are university graduates, but are educated fools. They make foolish decision, and their spiritual lives are filled with evil desires. Wisdom calls to us when we are driving on the road, or walking through the supermarket: who will listen to me? Wisdom is crying out in decisions about relationships–who should I date or not date? Wisdom speaks as we study at university–should I accept these theories as taught by a secular university? Wisdom cries out in every human relationship–when we meet in cell-groups or in fellowship together–saying, don't gossip, don't slander, don't show off, don't show that you feel arrogant. Wisdom waves its hands at us: listen to me–love people, pray for those who disagree with you. Wisdom tells us not to waste time on things that are non-essential, unproductive, and trivial. Wisdom says, listen to me, pursue me, and you will obtain understanding; do not forget God's Word or stray from its teachings; wisdom will protect you, exalt you, lead you; and "it will give you the ornament of grace upon your head and present you with a crown of glory" (Prov. 4:11).

Dear brother and sisters, this is what we need above all else: wisdom from on high. God will give us wisdom if we only ask it of him. That is his promise, and he never makes an empty promise. What he promises, he will fulfill.

Moses connected "numbering our days on earth" with "a heart of wisdom." We are in the flow of time; our existence is directed by time. Time is never static, but is dynamic in its power. Time compels us forwards, not backwards. We move from infancy to childhood; from childhood to puberty; from puberty to adulthood; from adulthood to maturity; and from maturity to old age; and then we die.

We grow older with time; we change physically, emotionally, and mentally. Thus we need wisdom to know how to spend our time on this earth. A middle-aged lady said that she could not look at her face in the mirror because her beauty has faded with time. Wisdom says to her: cultivate the garden of your inner heart; fill it with beauty and virtues, even though your outward beauty may fade with time.

As time passes, our memory also fades. As a teenager, I used to brag about my mental capacity to memorize many things. I could remember the details of the books I had read; but now, I cannot remember one quotation from the books I have written. This is sad, but true. Wisdom says to me: don't take pride in your own works, but take pride in God's work. Is it not as part of God's work that you have written these books? Move on, and continue to thank God for his gifts. Time has no mercy on our mental capacities; but wisdom says: God's mercy always abides, despite the changes and challenges that are facing us.

When my father-in-law died, he was 75 years old. I asked him for advice, for something that I could share in his memorial service. He told me: "To God, give thanks in all; to all people, show gratitude." The essence of life is not measured by its length, but by the quality and content of that life. Wisdom aims at quality, not quantity; wisdom is marked by praiseworthy acts, not by superficial deeds or so-called contributions. What are praiseworthy acts in life? (i) Revere God and give him thanks always; (ii) in ministry, do everything as we would do it unto God; (iii) with people, give and forgive, without asking for rewards or anything in return; (iv) to the world, share God's love and our love with them, even when you are rejected. These are the essentials of life on which wisdom must focus, and God will exalt you.

The need for God's forgiveness

Moses prayed for the grace of forgiveness because he needed it. Verse 13 reads: "Return, O Lord, how long will it be? Have compassion on thy servants." In other words, have sorrow or sympathy for our wrongdoings. The older Moses became, the more he was cognizant of his own heart. He was deeply aware that his heart was wicked beyond measure and deceitful above all things. Being conscious of the corruption or curvature of his own soul, he felt that God had forsaken him, that God was so, so far away from him. So he prayed humbly: "O Lord, how long will you stay away? O Lord, it is too long; O Lord, you are too far away, and too far away too long; I cannot stand it anymore. Come back to me; don't leave me here in my mess; don't allow my sin to keep condemning me; don't let me suffer the guilt of my own iniquities. O Lord, I want your forgiving grace. I want your intimate presence. O Lord, don't hide your face from me, and hide in the distance, beyond reach." It is this earnest prayer that opens heaven's gates, for it reaches into and penetrates the merciful heart of heaven. Grace begins to pour down from heaven like a shower of blessings, the grace by which we are cleansed and made free again.

How often when we feel God's absence, or think that God is far away, do we cry out like Moses did, "O Lord, return to me, sooner and quicker"? Do we not want to be cleansed again or freed again? If we do, then we should crave these things, and God will come upon us with a fresh, forgiving grace.

Because we truly need God's forgiving grace, we need to pray as Moses did: "O Lord, don't deal with me according to my sins." If he did, none of us could stand against his holiness. Who of we sinners can withstand the wrath of God against us? O Lord, don't stay at a distance; return to me, O Lord; don't come upon us with your judgment, but with your forgiving grace, because we need this more than anything else. Without the coverage of God's merciful, forgiving grace Moses could not live freely. So it is with us.

Grace always runs downhill, never uphill. When we seek to climb above God, grace is thwarted; but when we humbly seek his merciful face because we need it, then we will be surrounded by his forgiving grace. However, when God sees our arrogance, our carefree attitude, and a self-sufficient mindset, he hides his face from us. God resists the proud, but gives grace to the humble. He attunes his ears to the seekers, and those who seek shall surely find him.

The need for the immediate satisfaction of receiving God's love

Verse 14 says: "Satisfy us early in the morning with your unfailing love, that we may sing for joy and be glad all our days." This prayer reveals Moses' need of God's unfailing love, even as an older man.

Satisfaction–who doesn't need it? Unfortunately, we often look for satisfaction in the wrong places. We look for it in power, fame, wealth, drugs, alcohols, illicit sex, and things that don't please God at all. In contrast, Moses finds true satisfaction in God's love.

Human Needs and God's Provision (Psalm 90:12–17)

The older we get, the more we find ourselves in need of love. This should motivate us to assure our elderly parents continually that we do love and respect them. But more than this, we need God's love, which is far stronger than human love. Human love may fail, but God's love never fails. God's love is beyond understanding, and is unfailing love. Moses realized that the older he became, the more he needed the immediate satisfaction of God's love. He said, "early in the morning," not late at night. Consequently, his heart leaped for joy all his days. No wonder the philosopher Victor Hugo said: "The supreme happiness of life is the conviction that we are loved." Young people cannot wait to fall in love. When they are in love, they sing for joy. Being loved is a lovely thing, a blessed thing, and a joyful thing. And we all become better, stronger, and more cheerful people precisely because of love, especially God's love. "O Lord, satisfy me right now so that I may sing for joy."

There was a family from China. The parents held PhDs, and were trained in engineering. Due to language and cultural barriers, they could not find decent jobs in Canada. Their two daughters grew up and did very well in university. The father was so depressed for a long time that he contemplated suicide several times, but to no avail. I went to visit with him in his hospital bed. I reasoned with him: "You are being foolish–an intelligent man with a PhD would not end his life simply because there are no satisfactory jobs; there are still many satisfying things in life, like your adorable and gifted daughters who love you so dearly. Your children have never once complained about their lot, have they? They find contentment in the comfort and presence of their parents. What your children need is your love in the midst of their trials, difficulties, and losses."

I told him: "When your heart is without God, you become powerless, because when God is absent from your heart, the powerful love of God is missing. Where the most satisfying and most powerful thing in the world–God's love–is lacking, emptiness and powerlessness abound."

He later became a Christian, and lived a joyful life. All of us need love, but we need the kind of love that will never fail, which is God's love. As Charles Spurgeon said, "If you cannot trust God's hands, trust his heart." For the heart of God is so wonderfully kind and loving. I challenged this father to open his heart, and the love of God filled his heart; ever since, he has been singing and praising God every day, even though he continues to work as a waiter in a restaurant. He keeps saying to his guests: "The most satisfying thing in the world is to have God and his unfailing love in our hearts." The hymn writer was right to say:

> The love of God so rich and pure,
> How measureless and strong;
> It shall forever more endure,
> The saints' and angels' song.

The need for joy in the midst of affliction

Moses needed joy, and so he prayed, "O Lord, make us glad amidst pain and affliction" (v.15). When Moses wrote this Psalm, the people were nearing the end of the forty years wandering in the wilderness. During these 40 years, Moses experienced pain; he had seen death and dying, sicknesses, violence, danger, and every negativity in life. Because of their sin, the people of Israel spent 40 years wandering in the wilderness. In the Tsunami, there were approximately 50,000 deaths; in the 40 years of wandering in the wilderness, there were at least one million deaths. These days were filled with weighty afflictions and painful sufferings. Sorrows like sea billows rose, stripping them of every joy in life. Thus Moses cried: "O Lord, we have had enough pain; too long suffering; too much to handle; I cannot handle it; please make me lift up my head, and give me a cheerful countenance. Give me joy, a joy that is in proportion to the affliction. I cannot stand it; it has been too much for too long. Make me glad."

We need joy as we undergo trials and temptations. Let us learn to cast all of our cares and anxieties upon God, the source of every joy.

A story was told of two boxes–one black and one white. God told a lady: "cast all your sorrows and worries into the black box." So everyday she put all her worries and cares into the black box. God then said to her: "Put in it all the joys, successes, and all the goodness of your life into the white box."

After some time, she expected the black box to be heavier than the white box because she had been through so much pain and sorrow. But on the contrary, the black box was much lighter than before, and certainly lighter than the white box. She wanted to find out why this should be. Then she discovered that at the base of the black box there was a hole out of which the sorrows and cries fell. She cried: "Where have all these cries and sorrows gone?"

God replied: "Where? They are all here with me. I carry them, and that is why the black box is lighter."

She said: "Lord, I don't understand. Why did you give me two boxes?"

God replied: "Well, the black box I gave you to let go of your sorrows and cares; while the white box allowed you to count your many blessings."

God will make you glad; perhaps your black box feels too much to handle, too heavy to carry. God says: "Don't carry your cares with you; let them go; let me do this for you, and you will be filled with gladness, even amidst your difficulties." Always remember the white box: count your blessings, name them one by one, and see what God has done. Once you know how much God has blessed you, you too will be filled with joy. You will be empowered by joy to keep persevering, even amidst trials.

The need for God's continual work

Moses prayed for God's work to continue. In verse 16, he says: "Let your work appear (be seen or be manifested) not only in your servants, but also in the children of next generations." Moses was extremely anxious that God's work should continue, since without this we cannot work at all or accomplish anything. Moses is in great need of God, and God's redeeming work.

Moses knew how imperfect his own performances were; he knew that one day our work would come to an end. Like Moses, we will grow old, grow weaker; we may be incapacitated by illness, so that we cannot work anymore. But this will not prevent God from doing his work. Even when our works cease, our labor fails, and our performances falter, God's work will remain; his work must continue now and forever, unlimited by time and space.

Moses saw God working in his generation; but God's work should not stop there. Therefore he pleaded with God to continue working in the next generations. Even when our works are often inadequate, God's work is always effective, and will not stop; he will continue to accomplish his purposes in spite of human frailties or failures. Moses believed in the power of God's work; he needed God to act, and he wanted God to continue working with his people.

O Lord, let us see your work in our churches, in our offices, in politics, in schools and universities, in every aspect of our lives, that we may manifest your glory. Let us see your work so that our works may proceed out of yours. Without God's involvement, our labor may not bear fruits. O Lord, work in us, especially in the children of the next generation. The latter part of verse 16 reads: "Let your glory (the totality of God himself) be revealed to the children of the next generations." O Lord, enable the children of the next generation to perceive your glory; let them receive you into their lives as we have done in our generation. We need God to help us to perceive God and to receive God. O Lord, so work in our children that they are able to behold your glory, encounter you, and taste your goodness as we have done. Notice Moses' focus: "the children of the next generation." Pray that children will come to know God earlier, and will follow the path of righteousness.

How should we pray for children? I have three suggestions: (a) pray simply, (b) pray shortly, and (c) pray frequently for our children, teenagers, and young professionals that they will commit their lives to God, love God, and worship God alone.

The need for divine favor

Moses needs the beauty of God to shine upon him. Therefore he prayed in verse 17: "O Lord, may your favor (beauty) shine upon us." May your loveliness, may your glowing face shine upon us. How I need the face–shinning face–of God to shine upon me, my family, and my work! When I know that God's face glows towards me, I am lifted out of my depression and anxieties. I hunger for divine beauty, for his approving and shining face.

There is a Chinese saying, that your face reveals your hearts. If you give me a sour-apple look, then I am not well-liked by you; if your face shines when I talk to you, then your heart is warm towards me –you have me in your heart, and thus you smile. O God, let your smiling face shine upon me so that I could be embraced by your warm heart. What Moses desires is God's friendly or well-disposed regard for him, charged with great warmth and earnestness of emotion.

A little boy was caught in thunder and lightning while walking home from school. Each time the lightning flashed, he stopped and smiled at the light. The neighbors asked him with curiosity: why did you stop and smile as you did? He replied: "Well, each time the lightning comes, it is God taking a picture of me. God takes photo of me from heaven, and I know that he likes me. With each flashing light, God takes notice of me. God smiles at me and I smile back; and I am happy." What a wonderful answer! Yes, God takes note of us, every aspect of us. It does not matter where I am, whether I am up or down, in tears or fears, I need God's smiling face shining upon me.

I remember when my boy was four years old, he first learnt to jump into the swimming pool. He said to me: "Dad, when you are here to see me jump, I do much better. Would you come earlier to see me jump and splash water on the instructor?" So I came earlier, and I shouted to him: "Hansel, jump." I cheered him on: "Jump! You can do it." He did, and he received the biggest applause from the crowd. The instructor said: "Your son refused to jump until he saw your cheerful face and cheering voice. That was the best, most courageous jump ever." Children need the smiling faces of their parents to cheer them on; we too should desire the loveliness of God's face shining upon us. We need this and are better and stronger because of it. May the beauty of God's face shine upon all of you–that is a necessary prayer and a realistic prayer.

The need for God's affirmation of our labor

Finally, Moses prayed in verse 17b: "O Lord, establish the work of our hands; yes, establish the work of our hands." Look at the double emphasis: "establish the work; yes, establish the work." The final prayer is for a double portion of God's grace, through which our labor may bear fruit, last, and be found pleasing to God. If God's hand is not in our works, there will be no fruit. All labor is done in vain, were it not for God's grace. Deep down in all of our hearts, we need God's grace to sustain our labor.

We need a double portion of grace to accomplish the works that God has given us. Remember this: the "work" that Moses has in mind is a general term for all work, and should not be confined specifically to the pastoral ministry. It includes all kinds of works: being a grandmother, a teacher, a student, the president of a company, a full-time mother, a pastor, any kind of work that we are doing.

We must each dignify the work entrusted to us. Our labor should include certain types of attitude that are pleasing to God: (i) we must have a diligent attitude while working, as God does not bless laziness; (ii) have a sincere attitude, for God does not bless the hands of a hypocrite; (iii) enjoy the work entrusted to you. How can we enjoy our work? By not cursing the work given us, not complaining while we work. The ability to work is a gift of God. Imagine you were completely handicapped, unable even to bring yourself a glass of water. We should not curse or complain when we are able to work, whatever that may be.

A secretary recently retired from a big company, and I asked her, "What now?" She answered with joy and pride: "I am going to be a full-time grandmother. At least four grandchildren will be left under my full-time care for my love and protection. I am really looking forward to doing that." What an attitude of willingness to give herself to her grandchildren! I said to her: "May God richly establish the labor of your hands!" She replied loudly: "Amen!"

Finally, whatever we do, even in the little things, we should do them with great love. St. Theresa advised: "We don't do great things for God, but we should do little things with great love." God will establish our labor that is done with great love, even when our deeds are small.

With these proper attitudes, God will give significance to our work that is done with diligence, sincerity, delight, and with great love. The work that we do, in due time, will bear fruit. This is the manifestation of God's confirmation and affirmation of our doings. To God be the Glory!

8

Living with Style
(Philippians 4:1-9)

I remember preaching once in a church in India. After introducing me as the guest preacher, the pastor asked his congregation a straightforward question: "How many of you desire to live your Christian life with style?" That was his way of saying, "How many of you want to live a life of Christ-likeness? Nearly every single hand went up. They all wanted their life to be stylish, to be so filled with quality and beauty that others would be drawn to the God we worship.

St. Paul exemplified a stylishness that is worthy of our emulation. Philippians 4:1–9 provides several practical pointers for us.

First, to be stylish is to be affirmative of others (v. 1)

Paul said in verse 1: "My beloved brethren, you whom I love and I long for, you are my joy and crown." When Paul wrote this epistle, he was in prison. He was in a very difficult period of his life. Yet he did not allow his personal circumstances to get in the way of serving others. He moved beyond his immediate, persecuted context, and with heartfelt affection, he said: "My beloved ones, I am very proud of you; you are my joy and crown." That is stylishness–to be concerned about others in spite of one's personal struggles.

Could you imagine what Paul's affirmation might do for the people at Philippi? It made them feel worthy, glad, and strong.

Everyone you see has an invisible sign around his neck that says, "make me feel important." William James, the psychologist, said correctly: "The greatest need of humanity is the need for significance." I have learnt, mainly through failure, that friendship will never last if we only make others feel stupid and incompetent about themselves. The more I try to affirm the dignity and worth of others, the more friendships blossom, and others are built up. They feel stronger and happier than before.

Queen Victoria of Great Britain had two world-renowned prime ministers during her reign. Their names were William Ewart Gladstone and Benjamin Disraeli. Someone asked her to compare the two leaders. She said: "When I am with William E. Gladstone, I am *with* the world's greatest leader; however, when I am with Benjamin Disraeli, I *am* the greatest leader in the world." She stood tall because Benjamin Disraeli made her feel worthy and great about herself.

When people come near us, do they feel that we are affirming them? Or do they feel that we are belittling them or undermining their character? If that is the case, then we are not being stylish.

Stylish living means pouring our energy into making others feel worthy and stand tall.

Secondly, living with style means living with reconciliation as our aim, not division between people, especially for leaders (vv.2–5)

Two female leaders, Euodia and Syntyche, were not on good terms. The nature and content of their conflict is unknown. However, Paul clearly loved them both, and he desired them to be in harmony in the Lord. He said in verse 3: "Like other fellow-workers, their names are in the book of life." Oh yes, they disagree, just as men do; they have weaknesses as men have. But they are not evil women. Paul said they were his "true comrades," who shared in his struggle for the cause of the gospel. He urged the Philippian believers to help these two women to agree and to become united in the Lord. Paul's appeal is for harmony, not division; reconciliation, not hostility. Paul's exhortation is to be gentle in reconciliation, as he wrote in verse 5: "Let your gentleness be evident to all."

Mrs. Oliver Kenzo and Mrs. Ann Danier worked together as missionary nurses in South America. Both women were very strong leaders at a certain clinic. They loved the Lord, and were willing to give their lives to help the needy. However, they differed significantly concerning the policy of running the clinic. Together with the Council members, these two godly women discussed and argued for what they considered to be the proper way. Finally, the Council went with Danier's proposal. This decision tore them apart. Mrs. Kenzo found it hard to cope with the fact that she had lost the support of the Council. However, she overcame her inner battle, and humbly supported Mrs. Danier. She did not speak evil of her; rather, with gentleness, she worked under her superior. She applauded Danier's intelligence and diligence. She stayed with her all the way until she was taken home. That is stylishness–a greatness of heart coupled with apparent gentleness made manifest in her dealings with the one with whom she had differed.

Thirdly, living with style means living prayerfully (vv. 6–7)

Paul said in verses 6–7: "Be not anxious for anything, but in everything by prayer and supplication with thanksgiving let your requests be made known to God."

In petition, when we pray for something, God should be speaking for us; in intercession, he does something through us; and in communion with God, he does something in us, resulting in a heart filled with gratitude towards God. We draw near to God with our petitions and thanksgivings; we tell him our struggles, our hidden tears and fears, our broken dreams and lost hopes; we make our requests and needs known to God, and he cares for us.

Prayer is not an expression of an outmoded piety. Even in this scientific age, prayer is never outlandish, never irrelevant. It is never out of style, but is as contemporary and trendy as the latest fashion. Prayer goes up, power comes down, and the peace that surpasses all understanding floods our souls. The hymn writer was right to say: "O what peace we often forfeit; O what needless pain we bear; all because we do not carry everything to God in prayer." Everything? Yes, everything.

Martin Luther put this strongly: "To be a Christian is to pray." Prayer acts as oxygen for our souls, and so Luther advised: "Pray shortly, simply, and frequently." Prayer is never out of style. It is still the most effective weapon against evil and temptation. Be in prayer, and God "shall guard your hearts and your minds in Christ Jesus" (v.7).

Fourthly, living with style is living with a sanctified mind or godly imagination (vv.8–9)

Look at verse 8: "Finally, brothers, whatever is true, noble, right, pure, lovely; whatever is admirable, if anything is excellent or praiseworthy, think about such things." In other words, we should concentrate our minds on these virtues, the opposite of vices.

We often say that education governs the way we think. Indeed, it does. On the other hand, McNeil Dixon averred that the most powerful factor forming our character is imagination. Imagination rules all our lives. It is by imagination that we live, he argued, because the human mind is not a debating hall, but a picture gallery.

Imagination–we all have it. We should want an imagination that is godly, holy, and sanctified.

I have to admit that I do not like having my photo taken. None of the photos represents my true self. I recall when I was a teenager, I had to take twenty pictures in order to select one as a graduation picture. The studio manager almost kicked me out of his store. I said: "Don't you want to earn money?" With anger, he replied: "Yes, but not your money."

Even though I do not like having my photo taken, I do like taking mental pictures. I can remember vividly memorable events, lovely people, and edifying conversations. I imprint them in my mind. I aim to keep good and saintly pictures in my mental gallery.

We know that, in this day and age, we are not supposed to advocate censorship. People are free to watch and read anything they like. But isn't it sad that people feed their minds and imaginations with that which is debasing, destructive, and ugly? Isn't it sad that there are so many scenes of sex and violence on TV and in the newspapers? These images are constantly bombarding our minds. They affect us, especially the younger generation. Somehow, these images begin to shape people according to their ugliness. The apt words of Frank Outlaw apply to the discipline of mind:

> Watch your thoughts, they might become words;
> Watch your words, they might become actions;
> Watch your actions, they might become habits;
> Watch your habits, they might become character;
> Watch your character, it might become destiny.

Living with style involves disciplining ourselves to behold the beauty, not the beast; to embrace goodness, not evil; to desire purity, not ugliness. What kind of picture is hanging on your mental gallery? Cultivate a godly imagination, and you will be shaped according to the beauty of godliness.

We need to practice what we have learnt and seen in an exemplary leader like St. Paul (v.9), so that people will sit up and say: "That is stylishness. That is so much like Christ."